INTRODUCTION TO GROUP DYNAMICS

Introduction
to Group
Dynamics

MALCOLM AND HULDA KNOWLES

Revised Edition

Association Press
Follett Publishing Company/Chicago

INTRODUCTION TO GROUP DYNAMICS

International Standard Book Number: 0-695-81080-4
Library of Congress Catalog Card Number: 78-63135

3456789/838281807978

PRINTED IN THE UNITED STATES OF AMERICA

Contents

6 / Contents

Foreword to the
Revised Edition

WHEN we wrote the first edition of *Introduction to Group Dynamics* in 1959, the National Training Laboratories had been in operation for just ten years, but its network of associates had spread throughout the institutional fabric of the Western World. And its technical language and unfamiliar techniques were producing reactions ranging from excitement to bafflement and hostility.

At that time, the Director of Association Press asked us to write a small book that would help bridge the gap between the social scientists and the practitioners of group leadership. We recognized the need but were humbled by the magnitude of the task. And so we wrote the book in the spirit of trying the impossible, and expected that its usefulness would be limited and temporary.

We have been surprised and pleased, therefore, that

7

the demand for the book has increased each year. But, since the book's first appearance, many developments have occurred in the field of group dynamics, and it seems appropriate to prepare this revised edition to bring the subject up to date. To underline this statement, we need only cite the "Bibliography of Publications Relating to the Small Group" by Bertram Raven, sponsored by the Group Psychology Branch of the Office of Naval Research, which listed 5156 items in 1969. It would seem that there is an embarrassment of riches for students of group behavior. We hope that this new edition will help chart a course through these enlightening readings.

MALCOLM and HULDA KNOWLES

Orientation

How NOT to Read This Book

WE open on a negative note for a reason. Too often we ourselves have read simple books on complicated subjects with the false expectation that they would provide a short cut to expertness. We want to avoid any danger that you will be unrealistic about what you can expect to get out of this book.

Our mission in the book is modest, but, we believe, important. It is to paint a panoramic picture, in broad sweeping strokes, of the new and complicated field of group dynamics. Our purpose is to help you see it in perspective and grasp its main ideas. We hope to acquaint you with the language you will find in research reports about group dynamics sufficiently to give you a running start in reading them—for the social scientists use words that are not in the everyday vocabulary of many of us, both because they are describing concepts that are new and because they are trying to be scientifically precise.

We do not propose to try to provide a comprehensive analysis of the findings of the research into group behavior (that would require an encyclopedia). Nor do we set out to provide a manual of practice. This is not a "how to do" book but rather a "how to find out" book.

We hope that you will finish this book feeling that it has opened new horizons for understanding yourself and your fellow man, and wanting to probe the scientific literature that explores these horizons. We'll try to help you get started.

INTRODUCTION TO GROUP DYNAMICS

1

What Is Group Dynamics?

FIRST, a few words about what group dynamics is *not*. Because it is such a new field of study, some misconceptions have arisen about it. One misconception is that it is a well-organized school of thought or cult, with exclusive membership and a program of social action. It is not. Another misconception is that it is a technique or way of doing things. Thus, we have heard people talk about "the group dynamics method" —a phrase that, as we shall see, is really meaningless. A third misconception is that group dynamics is a doctrinaire approach to social organization which advocates "groupthink" over individualism. Nothing could be farther from the truth.

Four Uses of the Term

If group dynamics is not these things, then what is it? The term has come to be used in four different ways:

1. In its most basic sense, it is used to describe something that is happening in all groups at all times, whether anyone is aware of it or not. "Group dynamics" used in this way refers to the complex forces that are acting upon every group throughout its existence which cause it to behave the way it does. We can think of every group as having certain relatively static aspects —its name, constitutional structure, ultimate purpose, and other fixed characteristics. But it also has *dynamic* aspects—it is always moving, doing something, changing, becoming, interacting, and reacting. And the nature and direction of its movement is determined by forces being exerted on it from within itself and from outside. The interaction of these forces and their resultant effects on a given group constitute its dynamics. In this sense, "group dynamics" is to groups what "personality dynamics" is to individuals. It is a phenomenon that occurs naturally; nobody invents it.

2. "Group dynamics" is also used to describe a field of study—a branch of the social sciences concerned with using scientific methods to determine why groups behave the way they do. In this sense, it is possible to speak of "the investigation of group dynamics" in the same way that it is possible to speak of "the investigation of nuclear energy." As a field of study, group dynamics employs the tools and personnel of several disciplines of the social sciences: notably social psychology, clinical psychology, psychiatry, sociology, anthropology, and education. It makes use of the research facilities of a number of universities. It

includes in its field of study the phenomena that occur in groups in industry, the military services, educational institutions, voluntary organizations, social agencies, and in local communities. It sets up hypotheses and then tests them, using such techniques as observation of laboratory and natural groups, interviews, questionnaires, and various kinds of tests. From its factual findings it seeks to develop classifications of group phenomena, theories, and general principles.

3. A third use of the phrase is in reference to the body of basic knowledge about group behavior that has accumulated from past research. It is in this sense that one would speak of "the findings of group dynamics." This body of knowledge is found in doctoral dissertations, articles in the journals of the social sciences, monographs, pamphlets, and a growing number of technical books.

4. Finally, "group dynamics" has come to be used to describe a growing body of *applied* knowledge, or technology, which attempts to translate the findings and theories of basic knowledge into practical principles and methods. Applied group dynamics is concerned with the use of knowledge about group processes. In this sense, it is possible to speak of "group dynamics principles" or "techniques based on group dynamics," but never of "the group dynamics method." There is, of course, a close relationship between basic and applied knowledge. As Kurt Lewin pointed out in 1944, "In the field of group dynamics, more than in any other psychological field, are theory and practice

linked methodologically in a way which, if properly handled, could provide answers to theoretical problems and at the same time strengthen that rational approach to our practical social problems which is one of the basic requirements of their solution." [1] * Nevertheless, in trying to understand group dynamics it is necessary to distinguish between the body of basic knowledge and the technology which is derived from it. It is important to realize, also, that the principles and techniques derived from it do not proceed from an ideological position regarding how groups *ought* to behave; rather, they grow out of scientific evidence that certain types of behavior under certain conditions produce predictable consequences. Thus, the literature of applied group dynamics ideally does not say, "Do this or that," but rather, "If you do so and so under certain conditions, such and such is likely to happen."

Historical Perspective

The group has always been an important means for the accomplishment of human purposes. First in the family, then the clan, the tribe, the guild, the community, and the state, groups have been used as instruments of government, work, fighting, worship, recreation, and education. Very early in this historical development men began to discover by trial and error that certain ways of doing things in groups worked

* All notes and documentations appear at end of text.

better than others, and so a body of folk wisdom began to accumulate regarding the selection of leaders, the division of labor, procedures for making decisions, and other group techniques. It is natural that in an era of struggle against natural and human enemies the major concern was with assuring disciplined subservience to leadership rather than with improving the ability of group members to work together creatively and co-operatively.

In view of the fact that man has worked with small groups during most of his life on earth, it is indeed surprising that groups have received virtually no scholarly attention until modern times. Most of the fleeting notice given the subject in earlier literature consisted either of the expression of intuitive ideas, as in the writings of Lao-tze, or of the didactic listing of rules for leaders to use in manipulating their subjects, as in Machiavelli's *The Prince*.

It seems almost an inversion of normal processes that man did not begin to study seriously the small group life with which he is most intimately familiar until after he had devoted centuries of thought to the larger, more remote, aspects of social organization. Moral philosophers, beginning with the ancient Chinese and Greeks, have been concerned with phenomena associated with the behavior of large collections of people. Beginning late in the seventeeth century there developed a stream of speculative thinking about the social nature of man and the relationship between individuals and collectivities that laid the intellectual foundation for the revolutions against tyranny that swept through Europe and America during the next two centuries. This speculative stream included such Europeans as Hobbes, Locke, Hume, Mill, Smith, Montesquieu, and Rousseau, and such Americans as Madison, Paine, Jefferson, and John and Samuel Adams.

The early sociologists, beginning with Comte and Spencer and their followers in the nineteenth century, narrowed the scope of speculation to the crowd, the mob, the public, and mass movements, with their attendant phenomena of fads, fashions, hysteria, and the like. One of the most influential lines of thought was developed by the French sociologist, Emile Durkheim, around the turn of the century. He became especially interested in the process of interaction and theorized that individual ideas are altered in the process of "psyche-social synthesis" that goes on in groups, and that thus a group product emerges that cannot be explained in terms of individual mental processes.

In the early part of the twentieth century Cooley, Mead, and Simmel speculated about the element of social control in small groups, with special interest in the social conditions under which the motivation of individuals is most effectively developed. Hare, Borgatta, and Bales point out that the theme of the social control of behavior also dominated most of the early experimental research, and go on to summarize this research as follows:

Among the earliest relevant experimental studies are those of Tripplett in 1898, concerned with a curious facilitating or "dynamogenic" effect that occurred when people were together and in competition rather than alone. The alone and together theme was given a new impetus in the early twenties by the experiments of F. H. Allport, and is still active today. The study of child development by first-hand observation is another important source of small group research which goes back at least to the turn of the century. . . . Terman's 1904 study of the "Psychology and Pedagogy of Leadership" among children . . . is classic in its foreshadowing of methods and themes that were to be developed later in the work of Goodenough, Anderson, D. S. Thomas, Pigors, and many others. Piaget's work on children's games is almost in a class by itself as an exemplification of the study of the small group as the creator and carrier of a sub-culture.[2]

In the early 1920's Eduard Lindeman challenged the speculative character of most of the sociological studies of the group and suggested an empirical method for the study of functional groups. Under this stimulus the first large-scale attempt to do research on group process was carried on in "The Inquiry," which is reported in Lindeman's *Social Education*. The interest of "The Inquiry" focused on processes used by small deliberative committees and conferences in the solution of large social problems.

Benne and Levit provide this concise summary of other research in the 1920's:

Under the influence of Dewey's analysis of the act of experimental thought, students of discussion groups and discussion method developed a conception of group process as problem-solving, and developed descriptions and prescriptions for effective group procedure around this central concept. Elliott and Sheffield are representative of this emphasis. . . .

Motivated by the same psychological and logical currents as Lindeman and Dewey, Follett, through her extensive work in diagnosing current human problems in political, social-welfare, and industrial settings, came to identify the quality, character, and conditions of participation as the focus for studies of group process and experience. Her emphasis on leadership of function, as opposed to leadership of position or personality, and her stress on integrative behavior as a way of resolving conflicts creatively have exerted continuing influence on both study and practice of group methods. . . .

In addition to these logical and psychological influences upon group studies in the 1920's, Freud began a continuing line of inquiry into group formation and control. Drawing from the intimate and frequently unconscious bases of cohesion and control in the family group, Freud stressed the emotional aspects of group leadership and group formation rather than the organization of members for conscious work.

Somewhat apart from these theoretical reorientations toward group study, more or less isolated empirical studies of particular groups or kinds of groups went on during the 1920's without much attention to the demands of any comprehensive theory or of theorizing as a component to the research. Kolb's attempt to characterize rural groups represented such empirical investigations from a sociological slant. And Watson's demonstration that groups are more effective than individuals in solving certain types of problems was an example of such early group studies on the psychological side.[3]

A large volume of fact-finding studies based on the "trait theory" of leadership was also spawned in this era of "empiricist rebellion." A number of investigators sought evidence in support of the theory that certain personality traits (such as self-control, common sense, judgment, justice, enthusiasm, tact, perseverance, courage, decisiveness) are common to all successful leaders. This line of study produced a large volume of data, but few conclusions, because there was little agreement on the common traits. Charles Bird analyzed about one hundred such studies and found that only 5 per cent of the traits mentioned were common to four or more investigations.[4] Other investigators, employing the tools of sociology, sought to discover *ideal types* of leaders for different situations or social structures, such as bureaucracies, labor unions, political parties, and the like. This line of investigation established the importance of situational factors, but was not otherwise especially fruitful.

The two decades surrounding World War II witnessed the emergence of more clearly defined theoretical approaches to the study of groups. It will help in understanding the literature of group dynamics to have an overview of the principal approaches developed in this era.

The foundation for a "field theory" of group behavior was laid by Kurt Lewin, who came to the United States in 1932 as a visiting lecturer at Stanford and remained when the Nazi coup made his return to Berlin impossible. In 1935 Lewin and a dedicated group of graduate students initiated a series of classic studies of group behavior at the University of Iowa's Child Welfare Research Station. This group moved in the mid-forties to the Massachusetts Institute of Technology to form the Research Center for Group Dynamics. Within a year after Lewin's death in 1947 the Center moved again, this time to the University of Michigan. This Center has exerted a powerful influence on the study of group dynamics through its field theoretical approach.

Field theory, which has been so productive in physics, makes the assumption that a group at any point of time exists in a psychological field that operates not unlike an electromagnetic field in physics. This field consists of a number of forces (or variables) that are affecting the behavior of the group. The direction and relative strength of these forces determine the direction and speed of movement of the group. It is the task of the social scientist to develop techniques of observation and measurement that will enable him to analyze these forces and state the laws governing their operation. According to Lewin:

> What is important in field theory is the way the analysis proceeds. Instead of picking out one or another isolated element within a situation, the importance of which cannot be judged without consideration of the situation as a whole, field theory finds it advantageous, as a rule, to start with the characterization of the situation as a whole. After this first approximation, the various aspects and parts of the situation undergo a more and more specific and detailed analysis. It is obvious that such a method is the best safeguard against being misled by one or another element of the situation.[5]

Lewin felt that it was especially important to make mathematical representations of psychological situations so as to assure strictness of logic, power of analysis, and conceptual precision. Accordingly, his writings and those of his followers are liberally sprinkled with mathematical formulae and geometric figures.

THE FACTOR ANALYSIS APPROACH

Exemplified by the work of Raymond Cattell and his associates at the University of Illinois, this approach seeks to determine the major dimensions of groups by identifying their key elements. "That is to say," according to Cattell, "one would measure a large number of groups on a large number of attributes and determine a decidedly more limited number of independent dimensions by which any particular group in a given population of groups could be most economically and functionally defined" [6] Cattell used the term "syntality" to define for the group what "personality" defines for the individual. He is especially concerned with the factors of energy, ability, and leadership.

THE FORMAL ORGANIZATION APPROACH

Concerned primarily with developing a satisfactory conception of organization and an understanding of the nature of leadership in formal organizations, this approach dominated the reseach conducted over a period of years by the Ohio State University Leadership Studies staff headed by C. L. Shartle. Its techniques emphasize observations of interactions in organizational systems and detailed descriptions of the formal organizational structure of the systems.

THE SOCIOMETRIC APPROACH

Developed by the psychiatrist, J. L. Moreno, and his early associate, Helen Jennings, this approach focuses on the social aspects of group life, especially the emotional quality of the interpersonal relationships among group members. The method that lies at the heart of this approach is the sociometric test, in which the group members indicate which of the other group members they would choose or not choose as friends, partners, teammates, and the like, in particular situations. The development of the psychological structure of groups can be traced from data obtained from sociometric tests.

THE INTERACTION ANALYSIS APPROACH

Pioneered by Robert F. Bales and his colleagues at the Harvard University Social Relations Laboratory, this approach asserts that the overt behavior of individuals in interaction with one another and their environment is the "ultimate stuff" of scientific study. Elaborate devices, including an electrical "interaction recorder," and laboratory rooms with one-way windows so that groups can be observed without disturbance, have been invented for measuring interaction in small groups.

THE PSYCHOANALYTIC APPROACH

The emotional—primarily unconscious—elements in the group process and their effects on personality growth are stressed in this approach. Its method consists chiefly of the analysis of carefully recorded experiences and case records. This approach deals largely, although by no means exclusively, with therapeutic groups.

This approach has traditionally consisted of the analysis of narrative records of group workers and the extracting of generalizations from series of case histories of groups. Social group work has been primarily concerned with personality development through group experience, although not in a therapeutic setting. Group workers have tended to be more interested in practice than in research, and so the volume of scientifically validated studies from this approach has not been great. In recent years there has been a shift in group work research from descriptive research to action-research "to ascertain the influence of the leader's behavior and other conditions on the interaction within the group and on the personality development of its members." [7]

The postwar decade was characterized by several other notable developments in the field. One was the proliferation of university research centers focusing specifically on group phenomena—including centers at Boston University, the University of Chicago, Columbia University, the University of Illinois, New York University, and Temple University, in addition to those identified in the preceding discussion of theoretical approaches.

A major milepost in the history of the group dynamics movement was the establishment in 1947 of the National Training Laboratories (later renamed the NTL Institute of Applied Behavioral Science).

Founded under the leadership of three associates of Kurt Lewin—Kenneth Benne, Leland Bradford, and Ronald Lippitt—and with the sponsorship of the National Education Association, the "NTL" became the fountainhead of much of the research and most of the training in applied group dynamics over the next two decades. Its summer laboratories, in Bethel, Maine, and at several other locations throughout the country, developed a network of trainers who provided the principal source of supply for the enormous expansion of human relations training that took place in industry, government, education, and social agencies during this period. A somewhat similar organization in London—the Tavistock Institute—performed a similar role for the British Commonwealth.

This period also produced several journals devoted almost exclusively to reporting basic and applied research studies on group dynamics. These included *Human Relations,* the *Journal of Social Issues, Sociometry,* and *Adult Leadership.* The scholarly and professional journals of the various social science disciplines began to give an increasing amount of space to similar scientific reports. The technical literature of the postwar period was further enlarged with the appearance of such major books as R. F. Bales' *Interaction Process Analysis* in 1950, Cartwright and Zander's *Group Dynamics: Research and Theory* in 1953, Alvin Gouldner's *Studies in Leadership* in 1950, Harold Guetzkow's *Groups, Leadership and Men* in 1951, Hare, Borgatta, and Bales' *Small Groups: Studies in*

Social Interaction in 1955, Lippitt, Watson, and West-
ley's *The Dynamics of Planned Change* in 1958, and
Stock and Thelen's *Emotional Dynamics and Group
Culture* in 1958.

The Modern Era

The 1960's and 1970's have been a period of great
ferment, expansion, and controversy in the field of
group dynamics. Several trends have seemed to characterize this era.

One distinct characteristic is the diffusion of research activity among a widening spectrum of institutions and disciplines. In 1959 we were able to list less
than a dozen university research centers producing
the bulk of the research reports. By the 1970's behavioral scientists were investigating group phenomena
in departments of psychology, sociology, education,
social work, psychiatry, anthropology, business admin-
istration, and communications in scores of universities,
as well as in corporations, government agencies, hos-
pitals, mental health centers, consulting firms, along
with independent centers such as the Western Behavioral Sciences Institute in La Jolla, California.

Two sets of competing trends strike us about the
direction this research has been taking. One set has
to do with methodology: on the one hand, there has
been a growing emphasis on precision of quantitative
measurement and statistical sophistication; and on the
other, a rebellion against the fragmentation and de-

humanization of human beings and their relations, and an insistence on a more holistic, creative, subjective, value-oriented approach to the study of man (a rebellion which manifested itself in the founding of the Association for Humanistic Psychology in 1961). The other set has to do with the nature of the phenomena being studied: the previous heavy emphasis on small group behavior has given way to a movement toward the dynamics of the individual and his "human potential" (including transpersonal potential) on the one hand, and a movement toward larger social systems and societal issues (with emphasis on the dynamics and strategies of change) on the other.

Another major characteristic of the modern era is the explosive growth in the volume of technical literature. For example, in analyzing the frequency with which articles relevant to the study of small groups were published between 1900 and 1953, Hare found that the growth rate was from 1.5 items per year in the first decade to 1.3 items in the second decade, 11.2 in the third, 21.0 in the fourth, 31.2 in the five-year period between 1940 and 1944, 55.2 between 1945 and 1949, and 152 items per year in the four-year period between 1950 and 1953.[8] A "Bibliography of Publications Relating to the Small Group" compiled by Raven in 1965 listed 3,137 articles and books,[9] while the 1969 edition listed 5,156 items.[10]

The number of technical journals carrying articles on small group research has greatly increased and broadened, as well. In the 1959 edition of this book we listed fourteen that were then giving prominent attention to group dynamics; in preparation of this edition we found major articles in forty-three journals.

A third characteristic of the modern era is the increasing attention being paid to the group dynamics movement and its offshoots by the popular mass media. We have personally seen articles—some of them sensationalized exposés, some of them serious attempts at interpretation—in *Newsweek, Time, Seventeen, Fortune, Playboy, The Wall Street Journal, The New York Times Magazine, Glamour,* and *Saturday Review.* No doubt this is an incomplete list. There has been at least one full-length commercial movie portraying (caricaturing?) an encounter group and dozens of educational films. We have seen sensitivity training, or variations thereof, worked into a number of commercial television series and commercials, and National Educational Television has produced two series on the subject. Three books have reached, or come near, the best-seller lists: *Joy: Expanding Human Awareness* by William Schutz in 1967, Rasa Gustaitis' *Turning On* in 1969, and Jane Howard's *Please Touch* in 1970. We understand that human relations training has been both condemned by the John Birch Society and widely adopted in the leadership training manuals of many Christian denominations. Thanks to this attention from our popular sources of information, most Americans know that groups are "in" in our modern culture, although relatively few of them yet understand what this is all about.

A fourth characteristic of the last decade has been the proliferation of uses of group techniques in education and training. Although group discussion has been a backbone technique of education since ancient times, the group dynamics movement spawned a wide variety of mutations of the species "group." Among the forms now appearing in the literature are: T-groups ("T" standing for "training"), encounter groups, marathon groups, sensitivity training, human relations laboratories, human potential centers, growth centers, gestalt therapy groups, sensory awareness groups, biodynamics, confluent education, microlabs, and organizational development programs. One or more of these forms of learning groups have been incorporated into the curriculums of many schools and colleges, the inservice education programs of government agencies and corporations, the leadership training programs of voluntary organizations, and the services of management consulting firms. Perhaps as many as two hundred privately operated "growth centers" have been established across the country (and the world) with group experiences that are open to the public for a fee. Group techniques are used extensively in mental health, drug addiction, and weight-control programs. If the 1970 census had asked how many people had been exposed to at least one of the above forms of group experience, our prediction is that the tally would have exceeded a million.

2

Understanding
Individual Behavior

GROUPS are, first of all, collections of individuals.
An understanding of the behavior of groups, therefore, has to start with an understanding of the behavior
of individuals. Much of the research about group dynamics is concerned with gaining a better understanding of the causes and dynamics of individual behavior
in groups, and students of group dynamics make
abundant use of findings about individual behavior
from related sciences, especially clinical psychology
and psychiatry.

Where would a person who wants to understand the
different kinds of variable forces that cause individuals
to behave the way they do in groups start his inquiry?
The starting point is to know what questions to ask
and then to know where to go in the literature of the
social sciences to find answers. We'll try to provide a
general study guide.

Life History Forces

One set of questions that must be asked has to do with the effect of an individual's past experiences in life. The findings of psychoanalytic research are an especially rich source of answers in this line of inquiry. They suggest that the attitudes, values, and habits developed in the first group in a person's life—the family—may strongly influence his feelings and behavior toward leaders and authority and toward other group members. He may act out in a group the drama of his family life: he may be either submissive or rebellious to a parent-figure; either a rival or a companion to brothers and sisters, and he may feel most at home in either a warm and co-operative atmosphere or one that is cold and antagonistic. In other groups to which he has belonged during his lifetime he has also learned responses and behavior. If a certain pattern of behavior brought the desired results or was comfortable in previous groups, he will tend to repeat that pattern.

This area of research also indicates that one effect of past experience is the development of certain fairly stable tendencies to respond to similar situations in consistent ways. For example, out of the theoretical work by Bion and the further research by Stock and Thelen comes the notion that personality tendencies (termed "valencies") especially relevant to group behavior include "fight, flight, pairing, and dependency":

. . . an individual who has a strong valency for fight

tends to express hostility freely in the group; a strong valency for pairing indicates a tendency to express warmth freely and to wish to establish close relationships with others; a strong valency for dependency indicates a tendency to rely on others for support and direction; and a strong valency for flight indicates a tendency to avoid, in some way, the interactive situation. Every person possesses some valency, in varying degrees, for each of these emotional modalities. Such tendencies reside in the individual and form part of an habitual or stable approach to group interaction.[1]

Forces Based on Psychological Needs

Another type of forces to which much research has been directed is what is often depicted as universal needs. The biological needs, such as food, water, rest, activity, and sex, are widely acknowledged. Less well understood are the psychological needs common to all human beings, which have been the targets of a good deal of research by psychologists and anthropologists. Although these needs are often given varying labels, they include such ideas as the need for security, the need for affection or response, the need for status or recognition, for belonging, for new experience, and so on. These needs are not of the same strength for all people, nor for one person at different points of time; each individual has his own unique pattern of needs at a given moment. Furthermore, there is a presumption that a given need may express itself in quite different types of behavior by different individuals or by the same individual in different situations. For example, every individual on entering a new group has a need for security about what is expected of him. In one instance this need might result in withdrawal or holding back until the new member gets his bearings. In another instance the need for security might result in the opposite behavior of protective overtalkativeness.

An important insight that comes from the study of psychological needs is that they are not appropriate subjects for moral judgment. It makes as much sense to blame a person for needing recognition as it does to blame him for being hungry when his stomach is empty. If his need for recognition is causing him to irritate the group by monopolizing the discussion or other attention-getting behavior, the fault is not in his needing recognition—we all need it—but in his not knowing how to get it in socially acceptable ways. This area of research does not suggest that laymen should go around making off-the-cuff diagnoses of other individuals' psychological needs. But by understanding that all behavior is caused, the way is opened for us to become more tolerant and accepting of other people's actions and thereby to react to them constructively rather than with irritation and rejection.

Associational Forces

Another set of forces influencing the individual's behavior is induced by what we might think of as his "invisible committees." Every person is associated with a multiplicity of population groupings, some by intent but many by no act of will. Some may be unorganized and vaguely defined—we are businessmen or workers, housewives or teachers, black or white, Protestants, Catholics, or Jews, Democrat, Republican, or Independent. Others may be more definite and specific —our family, our neighborhood, the League of Women Voters, the YMCA, the First Methodist Church, the Centerville Chamber of Commerce, the United Steel Workers, and so on. In a sense, every time an individual starts to make a move several invisible committees representing these affiliations are sitting behind him putting pressure on him to act in certain ways—indeed, often in conflicting ways. And when he acts, it is with the feeling that whatever he does is being judged by these "reference groups" according to their purposes, standards, values, and goals.

Forces from Goals and Ideologies

Another set of forces influencing an individual's behavior is tending to pull him rather than push him. These forces are his own goals, his own standards and values, his own perceptions of reality, his own fears, his own conceptions of what he is and wants to be. Though these forces have grown out of all the other influences in his life, they have been given a unique shape in the way he has put them together. They are the magnets of his private would. And when the chips are down, they may well be the most influential factor of all in determining his behavior. Some research suggests that when a situation permits a person to be himself—to act freely and with integrity—his behavior will be the most constructive and creative of which he is capable. It is when he is under goading pressures to be something other than what he is—to be alienated from himself—that he is likely to become a "problem personality." The writings of Erich Fromm and David Riesman are especially illuminating in this area of investigation.

Internal Processes

One early school of psychologists (the determinists) believed that an act of behavior was produced by the sum total of these forces at work on an individual at a given time—that in reality he had little control over what he did. But most psychologists now believe that these forces are processed through such components of an individual's personality as intelligence, personal values and standards, self-concept, habits, fears, and styles of coping, so that the behavior that ensues is in the direction of the individual's personal goals and beliefs.

Summary

This is, of course, an oversimplified picture of the personality dynamics of an individual. But it may serve as a provocation, if not an enticement, to dip more deeply into the scientific literature on individual behavior. You will want to explore at least two additional lines of inquiry: (1) What are the effects of the dynamic interplay of these forces on one another? (2) What is the role of the symbolic processes—reasoning, planning, intending, imagining, thinking—in producing behavior? And you will no doubt want to look for other types of forces omitted from this brief overview.

To summarize, the types of forces at work on an individual as he enters a group that are depicted in the psychological literature might be pictured graphically somewhat like this:

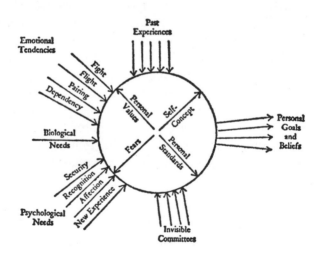

A full reading of the scientific literature along these lines of inquiry would not, however, provide a complete explanation of member behavior in groups, for there are some distinctly *group* variables which must also be taken into account, and on these we next turn our attention.

3

Understanding Group Behavior

A LEGITIMATE question to raise at this point is this: what happens when one individual, with his psychological field, gets together with other individuals with their unique psychological fields? How do they become a group with its own unitary psychological field?

What Is a Group?

The writers in the field of group dynamics do not agree completely on what distinguishes those collections of individuals that are groups from those that are not. But most of their disagreements are in emphasis and terminology. In general, they agree that a collection of people is a group when it possesses these qualities:

1. Definable membership—a collection of two or more people identifiable by name or type.
2. Group consciousness—the members think of

themselves as a group, have a "collective perception of unity," a conscious identification with each other.

3. A sense of shared purpose—the members have the same "object model" or goals or ideals.

4. Interdependence in satisfaction of needs—the members need the help of one another to accomplish the purposes for which they joined the group.

5. Interaction—the members communicate with one another, influence one another, react to one another.

6. Ability to act in a unitary manner—the group can behave as a single organism.

The essential differences between a collection of individuals that is a group and one that is not might be portrayed graphically like this:

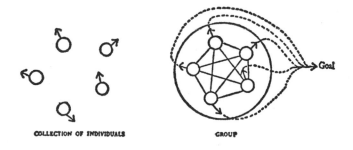

COLLECTION OF INDIVIDUALS   GROUP

In the collection that is not a group there are no shared goals—the goal arrows of the various individuals are pointing in different directions; there is no boundary around the collection, indicating a lack of consciousness as a group and undefinable membership; there are no lines of interaction and interdependence connecting the individuals; and obviously the collection is unable to act in a unitary manner.

Some Properties of Groups

There is such a profusion of kinds of groups in our nation of joiners that there appear to be few similarities among them. We can all name many groups to which we belong—the family, our social circle, the people we work with (and those special friends we go with on the coffee break), the infinite variety of committees we serve on at church, school, club, union, and in the community; and hopefully some study groups at the library, the Y, or the high school or college. In studying groups of all these types the researchers have identified certain properties or characteristics that all groups possess. These are the properties most commonly investigated and described:

1. *Background*. Each group has an historical background—or lack of it—which influences its behavior. A new group coming together for the first time may have to devote much of its early energy to getting acquainted with one another and with the group's task, as well as establishing ways of working together. On the other hand, a group that has met together often may be assumed to be better acquainted with what to expect from one another, what needs to be done, and

how to do it. But it might also have developed habits that interfere with its efficiency, such as arguing, dividing into factions, or wasting time.

Members come into a meeting with some expectations about it. They may have a clear idea of what the meeting is about, or they may be hazy and puzzled about what is going to happen. They may be looking forward to the meeting or dreading it; they may feel deeply concerned or indifferent. In some cases the boundaries around the group's freedom of action may be narrowly defined by the conditions under which it was created, or so poorly defined that the group doesn't know what its boundaries are.

These are merely illustrations of some of the elements that make up a group's background. Here are some questions that will help to provide an understanding of a group's background:

How well were the members prepared to enter the group?

What are their expectations about the group and their role in it?

What is the composition of the group—what kind of people, what is their previous experience, prior friendship patterns, and so on? How were they selected?

What arrangements have been made for their meeting—physical setting, resources, and the like?

2. *Participation pattern.* At any given moment every group has a particular participation pattern. For

instance, it may be all one-way, with the leader talking to the members; or it may be two-way, with the leader speaking to the members and the members responding to him; or it may be multidirectional, with all members speaking to one another and to the group as a whole. In a given group this pattern may tend to be quite consistent, or it may vary from time to time. The studies do not indicate that any one participation pattern is always best; it depends upon the requirements of a given situation. But many studies show that, on the whole, the broader the participation among members of a group the deeper the interest and involvement will be.

Some questions you may ask about a group to understand its participation pattern are these:

How much of the talking is done by the leader, how much by the other members?

To whom are questions or comments usually addressed—the group as a whole, the leader, or particular members?

Do the members who don't talk much seem to be interested and listening alertly (nonverbal participation), or are they bored and apathetic?

It is very easy, and often useful to a group, to chart the participation pattern during periodic segments of time, thus providing objective data about this aspect of its dynamics, like this:

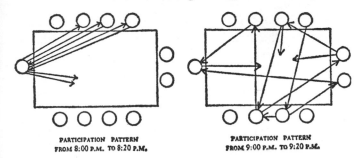

PARTICIPATION PATTERN
FROM 8:00 P.M. TO 8:20 P.M.

PARTICIPATION PATTERN
FROM 9:00 P.M. TO 9:20 P.M.

3. *Communication.* This property has to do with how well group members are understanding one another—how clearly they are communicating their ideas, values, and feelings. If some members are using a highly specialized vocabulary they may be talking over the heads of the rest of the group. Sometimes a group will develop a specialized vocabulary of its own, a kind of verbal shorthand, or private jokes that aren't understood by new members and outsiders.

Even nonverbal communication can often be eloquent. A person's posture, facial expression, and gestures, tell a great deal about what he is thinking and feeling.

Some questions that indicate the quality of a group's communications are these:

Are members expressing their ideas clearly?
Do members frequently pick up contributions previously made and build their own ideas on to them?
Do members feel free to ask for clarification when they don't understand a statement?
Are responses to statements frequently irrelevant?

4. *Cohesion*. The cohesiveness of a group is determined by the strength of the bonds that bind the individual parts together into a unified whole. This property indicates the morale, the team spirit, the strength of attraction of the group for its members, and the interest of the members in what the group is doing. In the literature it is often referred to as the "we-feeling" of a group. Symptoms of low cohesion include *sub rosa* conversations between pairs of members outside the main flow of the group's discussion, the emergence of cliques, factions, and such sub-groupings as the "old timers" versus the "newcomers," the "conservatives" versus the "liberals," and so on.

Questions about the group's cohesion include:

How well is the group working together as a unit?
What subgroups or "lone wolves" are there and how do they affect the group?
What evidence is there of interest or lack of interest on the part of members or groups of members in what the group is doing?
Do members refer to the group as "my group," "our group," "your group," "their group," or "his group"?

5. *Atmosphere*. Although atmosphere is an intangible thing, it is usually fairly easy to sense. In the literature it is often referred to as the "social climate" of the group, with such characterizations as "warm, friendly, relaxed, informal, permissive, free," in con-

trast to "cold, hostile, tense, formal, restrained." Atmosphere affects how members feel about a group and the degree of spontaneity in their participation.

Atmosphere can be probed by such questions as these:

Would you describe this group as warm or cool, friendly or hostile, relaxed or tense, informal or formal, permissive or controlled, free or inhibited?

Can opposing views or negative feelings be expressed without fear of punishment?

6. *Standards.* Every group tends to develop a code of ethics or set of standards about what is proper and acceptable behavior. Which subjects may be discussed, which are taboo; how openly members may express their feelings; the propriety of volunteering one's services; the length and frequency of statements considered allowable; whether or not interrupting is permitted— all these and many more "dos and don'ts" are embodied in a group's standards. It may be difficult for a new member to catch on to a group's standards if they differ from those of other groups he has experienced, since these standards are usually implicit rather than openly stated. Indeed, a group might be confused about what its standards actually are, and this may lead to much embarrassment, irritation, and lost momentum.

Questions about standards include:

What evidence is there that the group has a code of ethics regarding such matters as self-discipline, sense of responsibility, courtesy, tolerance of differences, freedom of expression, and the like?

Are there any marked deviations from these standards by one or more members? With what effect?

Do these standards seem to be well understood by all members, or is there confusion about them?

Which of the group's standards seem to help, and which seem to hinder the group's progress?

7. *Sociometric pattern.* In every group the participants tend very soon to begin to identify certain individuals that they like more than other members, and others that they like less. These subtle relationships of friendship and antipathy—the sociometric patterns—have an important influence on the group's activities. There is some research which indicates that people tend to agree with people they like and to disagree with people they dislike, even though both express the same ideas.

Questions which help to reveal the sociometric pattern are these:

Which members tend to identify with and support one another?

Which members seem repeatedly at odds?

Do some members act as "triggers" to others, causing them to respond immediately after the first members' comments, either pro or con?

8. *Structure and organization.* Groups have both a visible and an invisible organizational structure. The visible structure, which may be highly formal (officers, committees, appointed positions) or quite informal, makes it possible to achieve a division of labor among the members and get essential functions performed. The invisible structure consists of the behind-the-scenes arrangement of the members according to relative prestige, influence, power, seniority, ability, persuasiveness, and the like.

Questions to ask about structure include:

What kind of structure does the group create consciously—leadership positions, service positions, committees, teams?

What is the invisible structure—who really controls, influences, volunteers, gets things done; who defers to others, follows?

Is the structure understood and accepted by the members?

Is it appropriate to the group's purpose and tasks?

9. *Procedures.* All groups need to use some procedures—ways of working—to get things done. In formal business meetings we are accustomed to the use of *Robert's Rules of Order*, a highly codified and explicit set of procedures. Informal groups usually use much less rigid procedures. The choice of procedures has a direct effect on such other aspects of group life as atmosphere, participation pattern, and cohesion.

Choosing procedures that are appropriate to the situation and to the work to be done requires a degree of flexibility and inventiveness by a group.

Procedures can be examined through such questions as these:

How does the group determine its tasks or agenda?

How does it make decisions—by vote, silent assent, consensus?

How does it discover and make use of the resources of its members?

How does it co-ordinate its various members, subgroups, and activities?

How does it evaluate its work?

10. *Goals.* All groups have goals, some very long-range—for example, "to promote the welfare of children and youth"; others of shorter range—"to plan a parent education program for the coming year"; and others even more immediate—"to decide on a speaker for next month's meeting." Sometimes goals are defined clearly, specifically, and publicly, and at other times they are vague, general, and only implicit. Members may feel really committed to them or may merely go along with them. Since goals are so important to the group's ultimate accomplishment, they receive a good deal of attention in the literature.

Some questions about goals include:

How does the group arrive at its goals?
Are all members clear about them?
Are all members committed to them?
Are they realistic and attainable for this group?

Psyche and Socio Dimensions

The sociometric study of groups has illuminated another aspect of their character which, in turn, produces further insight about their functioning. In this analysis it appears at first sight that there are two completely different kinds of groups. Some of them, such as the bridge circle, the coffee gang, and the like, are highly informal, with few rules or procedures and no stated goals. People belong to them for the emotional satisfaction they get from belonging; they like the others, they are all friends. They tend to think of these groups as their social groups, but in the literature these are often called *psyche* groups. Membership in the groups is completely voluntary and tends to be homogeneous. The success of the psyche group is measured in terms of how enjoyable it is.

In other groups, however—committees, boards, staffs, and discussion groups—there are usually explicit goals and more or less formal rules and procedures. People tend to think of these groups, which exist to accomplish some task, as work or volunteer service groups. But in the language of social science they are *socio* groups. Their membership tends to be more heterogeneous—based on the resources required to do their work—and sometimes brought together out of compulsion· or sense of duty more than out of free choice. The success of the socio group is measured in terms of how much work it gets done.

As these dimensions have been studied more deeply it has become apparent that they do not describe different kinds of groups—few groups are purely psyche or socio—so much as different dimensions of all groups. Most groups need the psyche dimension to provide emotional involvement, morale, interest, and loyalty; and the socio dimension to provide stability, purpose, direction, and a sense of accomplishment. Without the dimension of work (socio) members may become dissatisfied and feel guilty because they are not accomplishing anything; without the dimension of friendship (psyche) members may feel that the group is cold, unfriendly, and not pleasant to be with. These dimensions of group life are dealt with most specifically in the writings of Helen Jennings.

Membership and Leadership Functions

Another aspect of group life that is crucial in understanding a group's behavior, diagnosing its problems, and improving its operation, is the way in which various required functions are performed. Kenneth Benne and Paul Sheats developed the following widely used classification of these functions: (1) *group-building and maintenance* roles—those which contribute to building relationships and cohesiveness among the membership (the psyche dimension), and (2) *group task* roles—those which help the group to do its work (the socio dimension). The first set of functions is required for the group to maintain itself as a group; the second set, for the locomotion of the group toward its goals.[1]

For example, some *group-building* functions are these:

Encouraging—being friendly, warm, responsive to others, praising others and their ideas, agreeing with and accepting the contributions of others.

Mediating—harmonizing, conciliating differences in points of view, making compromises.

Gate keeping—trying to make it possible for another member to make a contribution by saying, "We haven't heard from Jim yet," or suggesting limited talking-time for everyone so that all will have a chance to be heard.

Standard setting—expressing standards for the group to use in choosing its subject matter or procedures, rules of conduct, ethical values.

Following—going along with the group, somewhat passively accepting the ideas of others, serving as an audience during group discussion, being a good listener.

Relieving tension—draining off negative feeling by jesting or throwing oil on troubled water, diverting attention from unpleasant to pleasant matters.

And the following are some *task functions*:

Initiating—suggesting new ideas or a changed way of looking at the group problem or goal, proposing new activities.

Information seeking—asking for relevant facts or authoritative information.

Information giving—providing relevant facts or authoritative information or relating personal experience pertinently to the group task.

Opinion giving—stating a pertinent belief or opinion about something the group is considering.

Clarifying—probing for meaning and understanding, restating something the group is considering.

Elaborating—building on a previous comment, enlarging on it, giving examples.

Co-ordinating—showing or clarifying the relationships among various ideas, trying to pull ideas and suggestions together.

Orienting—defining the progress of the discussion in terms of the group's goals, raising questions about the direction the discussion is taking.

Testing—checking with the group to see if it is ready to make a decision or to take some action.

Summarizing—reviewing the content of past discussion.

These functions are not needed equally at all times by a group. Indeed, if a given function is performed inappropriately it may interfere with the group's operation—as when some jester relieves group tension just when the tension is about to result in some real action. But often when a group is not getting along as it should, a diagnosis of the problem will probably indicate that nobody is performing one of the functions listed above that is needed at that moment to move the group ahead. It seems to be true, also, that some people are more comfortable or proficient in performing one kind of function than another, so that they tend to play the same role in every group to which they belong. There is danger, however, in over-stereotyping an individual as a "mediator" or "opinion giver" or any other particular function, for people can learn to perform various functions that are needed when they become aware of them.

Often in groups one can observe behavior that does not seem to fit any of these categories. This is likely to be *self-centered* behavior, sometimes referred to in the literature as a "nonfunctional role." This is behavior that does not contribute to the group, but only satisfies personal needs. Examples of this category are as follows:

Blocking—interfering with the progress of the group by going off on a tangent, citing personal experiences unrelated to the group's problem, arguing too much on a point the rest of the group has resolved, rejecting ideas without consideration, preventing a vote.

Aggression—criticizing or blaming others, showing hostility toward the group or some individual without relation to what has happened in the group, attacking the motives of others, deflating the ego or status of others.

Seeking recognition—attempting to call attention to one's self by excessive talking, extreme ideas, boasting, boisterousness.

Special pleading—introducing or supporting ideas related to one's own pet concerns or philosophies beyond reason, attempting to speak for "the grass roots," "the housewife," "the common man," and so on.

Withdrawing—acting indifferent or passive, resorting to excessive formality, doodling, whispering to others.

Dominating—trying to assert authority in manipulating the group or certain members of it by "pulling rank," giving directions authoritatively, interrupting contributions of others.

The appearance of these behaviors in groups tends to be irritating to other members, and they tend to react to them with blame, reproach, or counterhostility. A group that understands group dynamics is often able to deal with them constructively, however, because it sees them as symptoms of deeper causes, such as valid personal needs that are not being satisfied constructively. Often, of course, it is difficult to place a given act in one or another of these categories

—what seems to be "blocking" to one observer may appear as "testing" to another.

The Role of Leadership

In this analysis of functions necessary to the performance of groups no distinction has been made between the functions of leaders and the functions of members. This is because the research fails to identify any set of functions that is *universally* the peculiar responsibility of the designated leader. But the fact is that groups in our society typically have central figures with such titles as "leader," "chairman," "president," and "captain." Ross and Hendry examine various theories that try to explain this institutionalization of the role of leader and, after assessing them as inadequate, give this view as to the current state of thinking:

> Perhaps the best we can say at this point is that any comprehensive theory of leadership must take into account the fact that the leadership role is probably related to personality factors, to the attitudes and needs of "followers" at a particular time, to the structure of the group, and to the situation. . . . Leadership is probably a function of the interaction of such variables, and these undoubtedly provide for role differentiation which leads to the designation of a "central figure" or leader, without prohibiting other members in the group from performing leadership functions in various ways, and at various times, in the life of the group.[2]

A classic series of experiments often quoted in the literature of group dynamics bears on leadership style. The experiments were conducted by Ronald Lippitt and Ralph White in the research program headed by Kurt Lewin at the University of Iowa in the 1930's. Their purpose was to measure as precisely as possible the effects of different types of leader behavior on a number of experimentally created groups of boys. The three types of leader behavior tested were "authoritarian" (policy determined by the leader), "democratic" (all policies a matter of group discussion and decision, encouraged and assisted by the leader), and "laissez-faire" (complete freedom for group or individual decision, with a minimum of leader participation). Their studies produced evidence for the following generalizations:

1. Authoritarian-led groups produced a greater quantity of work over a short period of time, but experienced more hosility, competition, and aggression —especially scapegoating, more discontent beneath the surface, more dependence, and less originality.

2. Democratically led groups, slower in getting into production, were more strongly motivated, became increasingly productive with time and learning, experienced more friendliness and teamwork, praised one another more frequently, and expressed greater satisfaction.

3. Laissez-faire groups did less work and poorer work than either of the others, spent more time in

horseplay, talked more about what they should be doing, experienced more aggression than the democratic groups but less than the authoritarian, and expressed a preference for democratic leadership.

A mounting body of research on the leadership role since World War II, especially that sponsored by the Office of Naval Research,[3] supports the thesis that some situations require authoritarian and others laissez-faire leadership, but that in the long run in normal situations groups thrive best when the leadership functions are democratically shared among the members of the group.

Groups in Motion

So far we have been looking at the complicated elements or variables that make up a group—its properties, dimensions, and membership and leadership functions—almost as if a group stood still in time and space. Actually, a group is never static; it is a dynamic organism, constantly in motion. Not only is it moving as a unit, but the various elements within it are constantly interacting. A change in procedure will affect atmosphere, which will affect the participation pattern, which will affect cohesion, which will affect leadership, which will affect procedure, and so on. Actually, most of the research has to do with the dynamic interaction of these variables in groups in motion.

There seems to be fairly general agreement among the students of group dynamics that groups move through more or less predictable phases of development during their life cycle. A number of theories about what these phases are have been proposed, as summarized, page 61. Notice that while each theory focuses on a different theme, they all indicate quite similar phenomena occurring in the early, middle, and later phases of group development.[4]

Some General Principles

The study of group dynamics is beginning to produce some generalizations or laws of cause and effect that make it increasingly possible to understand, predict, and improve group behavior. It would be impossible even to try to summarize the body of findings or "working hypotheses" that have accumulated from the research to date in a small book. You might be interested, however, in a sample of the general principles that seem to be emerging.

In this spirit we list below some of the principles that have been most helpful in understanding group behavior:

1. A group tends to be attractive to an individual and to command his loyalty to the extent that:
   a. It satisfies his needs and helps him achieve goals that are compelling to him.

	PHASE 1: Individually Centered	PHASE 2: Frustration and Conflict	PHASE 3: Attempted Consolidation of Group Harmony	PHASE 4: Individual Self-Assessment, Flexibility of Group Process, Emphasis upon Productivity in Problem Solving
Thelen and Dickerman (1949)				
Miles (1953)	PHASE 1: Unoriented, restive "talking about" irrelevant matters	PHASE 2: Abstract "talking about" Leadership and Permissiveness		PHASE 3: "Doing Level!"—Discussion and analysis of Here-and-Now
Bemis and Shepard (1956)	SUBPHASE 1: Dependence—Submission Phase I: Dependence	SUBPHASE 2: Counterdependence SUBPHASE 3: Resolution	SUBPHASE 4: Enchantment Phase II: Interdependence	SUBPHASE 5: Disenchantment SUBPHASE 6: Conceptual Validation
Schutz (1958)	PHASE 1: Inclusion		PHASE 2: Control	PHASE 3: Affection
Bion (1961)	STAGE 1: Flight		STAGE 2: Fight	STAGE 3: Unite
Golembiewski (1962)	PHASE 1: Establishing the Hierarchy	PHASE 2: Conflict and Frustration	PHASE 3: Growth of Security and Autonomy	PHASE 4: Structuring in terms of Work-Task
Bradford (1964)	STAGE 1: Ambiguity STAGE 2: Self-Investment Participation	STAGE 3: Collaboration and Learning from Peers	STAGE 4: Motivation for Learning	STAGE 5: Experienced Behavior and Feedback STAGE 6: Group Growth and Development
Mills (1964)	STAGE 1: The Encounter	STAGE 2: Testing Boundaries and Modeling Behavior	STAGE 3: Negotiating an Indigenous Normative System	STAGE 4: Production STAGE 5: Separation
Tuckman (1965)	STAGE 1: Forming—Testing and Dependence	STAGE 2: Storming—Intragroup Conflict	STAGE 3: Norming—Development of Group Cohesion	STAGE 4: Performing—Functional Role-Relatedness
Mann (1967)	PHASE 1: Initial Complaining	PHASE 2: Premature Enactment	PHASE 3: Confrontation PHASE 4: Internalization	PHASES 5 & 6: Separation and Terminal Review
Dunphy (1968)	PHASE 1: Counterpersonal and Negativity Maintenance of External Normative Standard	PHASE 2: Individual Rivalry and Aggression	PHASE 3: PHASE 4: Transitional—Negativity Membership Realization of Unattainable Utopian Ideals	PHASE 5: Emotional Concerns PHASE 6: End of Group

* For this graphic summary the authors are indebted to Gary Miller, a master's degree candidate in the Graduate Program in Adult Education at Boston University.

      b. It provides him with a feeling of acceptance and security.

      c. Its membership is congenial to him.

      d. It is highly valued by outsiders.

2. Each person tends to feel committed to a decision or goal to the extent that he has participated in determining it.

3. A group is an effective instrument for change and growth in individuals to the extent that:

      a. Those who are to be changed and those who are to exert influence for change have a strong sense of belonging to the same group.

      b. The attraction of the group is greater than the discomfort of the change.

      c. The members of the group share the perception that change is needed.

      d. Information relating to the need for change, plans for change, and consequences of change is shared by all relevant people.

      e. The group provides an opportunity for the individual to practice changed behavior without threat or punishment.

      f. The individual is provided a means for measuring progress toward the change goals.

4. Every force tends to induce an equal and opposite counterforce. (Thus, the preferred strategy for change, other things being equal, is the weakening of forces resisting change rather than the addition of new positive forces toward change. For instance, if a group in a factory is resisting

a new work procèdure, it may be because they
don't understand how it will work, in which
case a demonstration or trial experience will be
superior to exhortation or pressure.)

5. Every group is able to improve its ability to
operate as a group to the extent that it consciously examines its processes and their consequences and experiments with improved processes. (In the literature this is referred to as the
"feedback mechanism," a concept similar to that
used in guided missiles, which correct any deviations from their course while in flight on the
basis of data collected by sensitive instruments
and fed back into their control mechanism.)

6. The better an individual understands the forces
influencing his own behavior and that of a group,
the better he will be able to contribute constructively to the group and at the same time to
preserve his own integrity against subtle pressures toward conformity and alienation.

7. The strength of pressure to conform is determined by the following factors:
   a. The strength of the attraction a group has for
   the individual.
   b. The importance to the individual of the issue
   on which conformity is being requested.
   c. The degree of unanimity of the group toward
   requiring conformity.

8. The determinants of group effectiveness include:
   a. The extent to which a clear goal is present.

b. The degree to which the group goal mobilizes energies of group members behind group activities.

c. The degree to which there is agreement or conflict among members concerning which one of several possible goals should control the activities of the group.

d. The degree to which there is agreement or conflict among the members concerning means that the group should use to reach its goal.

e. The degree to which the activities of different members are co-ordinated in a manner required by the group's tasks.

f. The availability to the group of needed resources, whether they be economic, material, legal, intellectual, or other.

g. The degree to which the group is organized appropriately for its task.

h. The degree to which the processes it uses are appropriate to its task and stage of development.

4

Contemporary Research
in Group Behavior

IN 1953 Cartwright and Zander described the current status of the literature of group dynamics in these words:

> As one studies the various writings about groups, one is impressed with the multitude of different ways in which problems have been stated, the great variety of research methods that have been employed, and the confusion of tongues in describing what happens in groups. A first reaction might well be to become disheartened by the apparent chaos and disagreement. A more careful study of the field will reveal, however, that many of the apparently competing "theories" and "ex-

The authors wish to express their gratitude to Dan Hogan, a master's degree candidate in the Graduate Program in Adult Education at Boston University, for providing the structure and much of the material used in this chapter.

planations" do not actually contradict but rather augment and amplify one another.[1]

A decade later Stock described the situation this way:

> Research about T-groups suggests a large checkerboard, incompletely and unevenly filled in. Some areas show a considerable concentration of work; others are nearly empty. In some areas, the questions have been asked and answered. In others, the questions are clear, but methodology or relevant theory is not yet fully developed. In still other areas, even the questions are not yet well defined. To complicate the analogy, the checkerboard is expanding, and the issues which previously did not exist are constantly emerging in response to new applications and modifications of the T-group.[2]

The complexity of the group dynamics literature is partly the result of the many different kinds of groups used for research—school classes, factory teams, jet bomber crews, fabricated laboratory groups, and so on. Partly the confusion stems from the diversity of social problems that have motivated research, ranging from intergroup conflict to factory production. And partly it is a product of the interdisciplinary character of the field, with its ideas, methods, and terminology consisting of a potpourri drawn from psychology, sociology, psychiatry, anthropology, industrial relations, social work, education, speech, along with a pinch of political science and economics and even a periodic dash of mathematics and physical science.

As interest in group dynamics has burgeoned, so too has the research attempting to discover precisely what these dynamics are. The contemporary research literature seems to focus on three lines of inquiry: (1) the study of group variables and their effect on group and individual change; (2) the study of group and individual change as a result of group experience; and (3) the study of the process of group development. Let us explore the directions in which the researchers' curiosity has led them, citing some examples of typical studies as we go.

The Study of Group Variables and Their Effect on Group and Individual Behavior

Within this broad category of inquiry researchers have been curious to discover what differences in outcomes are associated with different types of groups, decision-making procedures, communications patterns, and other variables:

1. TYPE OF GROUP

   D. R. Bunker, "Individual Applications of Laboratory Training," *Journal of Applied Behavioral Science,* 1965, I, pp. 131–148.

   D. Hooper, A. Sheldon, and A. J. R. Koumans, "A Study of Group Psychotherapy with Married Couples, Part I: The Group Method," *International Journal of Social Psychiatry,* 1969, XV, pp. 57–68.

E. E. Mintz, "Marathon Groups: A Preliminary Evaluation," *Journal of Contemporary Psychotherapy,* 1969, I, pp. 91–94.

2. METHODOLOGY

L. Bolman, "Laboratory versus Lecture in Training Executives," *Journal of Applied Behavioral Science,* 1970, VI, pp. 323–335.

N. A. Polansky and E. B. Harkins, "Psychodrama as an Element in Hospital Treatment," *Psychiatry: Journal for the Study of Interpersonal Processes,* 1969, XXXII, pp. 74–87.

3. DECISION-MAKING PROCEDURES

P. R. Bell and B. D. Jamieson, "Publicity of Initial Decisions and the Risky Shift Phenomenon," *Journal of Experimental Social Psychology,* 1970, VI, pp. 329–345.

4. COMMUNICATION PATTERNS

R. F. Bales, *et al.,* "Channels of Communication in Small Groups," *American Sociological Review,* 1951, XVI, pp. 461–468.

5. LEADERSHIP INFLUENCE

A. Zander, H. Medow, and R. Efron, "Observers' Expectations as Determinants of Group Aspirations," *Human Relations,* 1965, XIX, 273–287.

C. L. Cooper, "The Influence of the Trainer on Participant Change in T-Groups," *Human Relations,* 1969, XXII, pp. 515–530.

6. AMOUNT OF TIME

D. R. Bunker and E. S. Knowles, "Comparison

of Behavioral Changes Resulting from Human Relations Training Laboratories of Different Lengths," *Journal of Applied Behavioral Science,* 1967, III, pp. 505–523.

7. GROUP SIZE

C. N. Zimet and C. Schneider, "Effects of Group Size on Interaction in Small Groups," *Journal of Social Psychology,* 1969, LXXVII, pp. 177–187.

8. GROUP COMPOSITION

B. D. Fine, "Comparison of Work Groups with Stable and Unstable Membership," *Journal of Applied Psychology,* 1971, LV, pp. 170–174.

9. FEEDBACK

F. A. Heller, "Group Feedback Analysis as a Change Agent," *Human Relations,* 1970, XXXIII, pp. 319–333.

10. GROUP STRUCTURE

J. O. Morrissette, *et al.,* "Degree of Structural Balance and Group Effectiveness," *Organizational Behavior and Human Performance,* 1967, II(4), pp. 383–393.

The Study of Group and Individual Change as a Result of Group Experience

This line of inquiry is concerned with identifying the types of changes produced through group experience and the variables that influence these results:

1. SENSITIVITY

   R. M. Bramson, "Changes in Social Sensitivity in Group Training," *Dissertation Abstracts International*, 1970, XXXI(2-A), p. 823.

2. SELF-CONCEPT

   R. D. McGee, "A Study of Sensitivity Training as a Method of Changing Self Concept," *Dissertation Abstracts International*, 1970, XXX (11-A), p. 4860.

3. SELF-AWARENESS

   J. V. Clark and S. A. Culbert, "Mutually Therapeutic Perceptions and Self-Awareness in a T-Group," *Journal of Applied Behavioral Science*, 1965, I, pp. 180–194.

4. CONGRUENCE

   D. R. Peters, "Self-Ideal Congruence as a Function of Human Relations Training," *Journal of Psychology*, 1970, LXXVI, pp. 199–207.

5. RISK-TAKING

   M. W. Belovicz, *et al.*, "A Critical Analysis of the 'Risky Shift' Phenomenon," *Organizational Behavior and Human Performance*, 1971, VI, pp. 111–131.

6. TASK EFFECTIVENESS

   S. C. Schiflett, "Prediction of Group Productivity as a Function of Member Ability, Task-Solving Strategy and Task Difficulty," *Dissertation Abstracts International*, 1970, XXXI(2-A), p. 830.

7. PROBLEM-SOLVING

V. H. Vroom, L. D. Grant, and T. S. Cotton, "The Consequences of Social Interaction in Group Problem Solving," *Organizational Behavior and Human Performance,* 1969, IV (1), pp. 77–95.

8. CONFORMITY

G. S. Rotter, "An Experimental Evaluation of Group Attractiveness as a Determinant of Conformity," *Human Relations,* 1967, XX, pp. 273–281.

9. POTENTIAL DANGERS

B. Lubin and M. Zuckerman, "Level of Emotional Arousal in Laboratory Training," *Journal of Applied Behavioral Science,* 1969, V, pp. 483–490.

L. A. Gottschalk and E. M. Pattison, "Psychiatric Perspectives on T-Groups and the Laboratory Method: An Overview," *American Journal of Psychiatry,* 1969, CXXVI, pp. 823–840.

The Process of Group Development

As was indicated in Chapter 3, there has been widespread interest among theorists and researchers in the developmental phases of group life and their effect on individual behavior and change. The "Summary of Theories of Phase Movement in Groups" on page 61 provides a convenient overview of ideas about the phasic movement of groups from the following sources:

W. G. Bennis and H. A. Shepard, "A Theory of Group Development," *Human Relations,* 1956, IX, pp. 415–437.

W. H. Bion, *Experiences in Groups* (New York: Basic Books, 1959).

L. P. Bradford, J. R. Gibb, and K. D. Benne, *T-Group Theory and Laboratory Method* (New York: John Wiley & Sons, 1964).

D. C. Dunphy, "Phases, Roles, and Myths in Self-Analytic Groups," *Journal of Applied Behavioral Science,* 1968, IV, pp. 195–225.

R. T. Golembiewski, *The Small Group* (Chicago: University of Chicago Press, 1962).

M. B. Miles, "Human Relations Training: How a Group Grows," *Teachers College Record,* 1955, LV, pp. 90–96.

T. M. Mills, *The Sociology of Small Groups* (Englewood Cliffs, N.J.: Prentice-Hall, Inc., 1967).

W. C. Schutz, *FIRO: A Three Dimensional Theory of Interpersonal Behavior* (New York: Holt, Rinehart & Winston, 1958).

H. A. Thelen and W. Dickerman, "Stereotypes and the Growth of Groups," *Educational Leadership,* 1949, VI, pp. 309–316.

R. D. Mann *et al., Interpersonal Styles and Group Development* (New York: John Wiley and Sons, Inc., 1967).

B. W. Tuckman, "Developmental Sequence in Small Groups," *Psychological Bulletin,* 1965, LXIII (6), pp. 384–399.

Overviews of Research

Several comprehensive overviews are available to guide an inquirer through the morass of research literature in this field:

Dorwin Cartwright and Alvin Zander, eds., *Group Dynamics Research and Theory* (Evanston, Ill.: Row, Peterson & Co., 1953).

A. Paul Hare, *Handbook of Small Group Research* (New York: The Free Press of Glencoe, 1962).

Dorothy Stock, "A Survey of Research on T Groups," in L. P. Bradford, J. R. Gibb, and K. D. Benne (eds.), *T-Group Theory and Laboratory Method* (New York: John Wiley & Sons, 1964).

National Training Laboratories, *Explorations in Human Relations Training and Research*: No. 1, "Problems in the Design and Interpretation of Research on Human Relations Training" by Roger Harrison; and No. 2, "A Bibliography of Research" by Lewis Durham, Jack R. Gibb, and Eric S. Knowles (Washington, D.C.: National Education Association, 1967).

5

Practical Applications

As is true of any field of fundamental research, many of the findings of research in group dynamics have practical implications. As Thelen states, "The aim of science is to describe nature and its laws. The aim of technology is to state policies by which man can control nature for stated ends. Technology is the set of ideas man uses in acting out his needs and in satisfying his purposes. As science develops and nature is understood better, technology also changes." [1] The fact is that the research into group dynamics has greatly influenced the technology of working with groups across a wide spectrum of social practice, as portrayed below.

This chart demonstrates a point made in Chapter 1: that "group dynamics" is not a particular ideology or a single technology; it is a field of study and practice that cuts across ideologies and technologies. At one end of the spectrum, the practice of psychotherapy has been greatly influenced by the insights gained from the group dynamics movement. Even the classical

SPECTRUM OF APPLIED GROUP DYNAMICS

PSYCHO-THERAPY	HUMAN RELATIONS TRAINING (EDUCATION)		SOCIAL ACTION
→	→	→	
Group therapy	Human Potential Movement	Encounter groups	Group process training	Organization development
Synanon		T-Groups		Change agent training
	Gestalt therapy		Leadership training	
Family therapy		Skill-training groups		
	Bio-energetics		Management development	Community change labs
Psycho-drama		Instrumented labs		
	Sensory awakening			
	Meditation	Conflict management labs		
	Marathons			
		Inter-group labs		

psychoanalysts have incorporated the findings of group dynamics research into their practice: the American Psychiatric Association and the National Institute for Mental Health have collaborated for several years on a continuing education program for psychiatrists in group dynamics. But some new psychotherapeutic techniques have also evolved from the group dynamics movement, such as Synanon groups (for drug addicts and convicts), family therapy groups, and psychodrama.

Straddling the continuum between psychotherapy

and education is the expansive human potential movement, with its focus on personal growth through gestalt therapy, bio-energetics, sensory awakening, meditation, marathons, and various forms of encounter groups. Moving on up the continuum farther away from an emphasis on personal emotional development toward increasing emphasis on conceptual and skill training are the NTL-type T-Groups, skill training groups (such as in communications, problem-solving, and decision-making), instrumented labs, conflict management labs, and intergroup relations labs. Toward the far end of the continuum are the social practices that are concerned with improving the quality of the work done in organizations and communities—organization development, change agent training, and community change (or development) labs.

Probably the greatest impact made to date by the group dynamics movement on the practical affairs of our culture has been in leadership training and organizational development.

Leadership (and Membership) Training

Traditionally, leadership training has consisted of selecting people with the right "traits" for leadership positions and then indoctrinating them with the particular knowledge and skills required for particular jobs, such as being chairmen of particular committees, leading particular types of discussions, teaching particular subjects, or managing particular organizations.

To this first dimension of leadership training have been added two new dimensions as a result of the research in group dynamics. The second dimension consists of generalized understandings of group behavior that are applicable to *all* groups in *all* situations. This second dimension might be thought of as the "liberal arts" program in leadership development, whereas the first dimension is more akin to the "vocational training" aspect of leadership development. The third dimension consists of training for all group members, not just the designated leaders, in the skills of group participation. It recognizes that leadership within a group often shifts as situations change and that in many respects the most effective training is done with the group as a whole in terms of its continuous experience.

The new technology of training emphasizes the development of an understanding of the forces at work in groups, the development of sensitivity to the needs of individuals and groups, the development of skill in diagnosing human relations problems, and the development of the ability to learn from actual experience. It starts with the proposition that the target of training is change in the behavior of individuals so that they can take appropriate and effective membership in groups. Bradford explains:

> This viewpoint necessitates looking at forces of resistance to change both within the individual and in his

total situation as well as at the process of changing. Instead of thinking about ways of "teaching" facts, it is necessary to analyze the conditions which keep the individual from changing, the requirements to help him change, and the supports necessary to help him maintain his change.[2]

This approach involves the diagnosing of the needs for change, the forces of resistance to change, and the motivations for change in each particular situation, and then designing a training program consisting of a number of elements and using many methods which will help the individual to bring about the changes he desires. Training designs typically make use of the following types of activity:

Laboratory groups. These are given a wide variety of labels, including "T-groups," "nondirective groups," "diagnostic groups," "sensitivity groups," "workshop groups," and "lab groups." A laboratory group provides participants with the experience of constructing without blueprint or direction an organism which has goals, structure, procedures, standards, and other elements of group life. The trainers do not tell the group what to do, but help them to analyze their behavior as they go about forming a group. Again in Bradford's words:

> The group provides an opportunity for trainees to behave, to secure feed-back on their behavior, to experiment with new ideas of leadership and membership

and to get—on the feeling as well as the intellectual level—a real awareness of the problems of group organization, functioning, and growth.[3]

Theory sessions. These are general meetings of all participants in which theories and research findings are presented through lectures, motion pictures, demonstrations, panel discussions, and other methods. Such topics as the following are treated: "Characteristics of Groups," "The New Member in the Group," "Concepts and Kinds of Leadership," "Roles in Effective Group Action," "Understanding Individual Motivation," "Human Factors Affecting Productivity," "Problem-Solving in Small Groups," "Some Basic Features of Social Systems," and "Communications in Formal Organizations."

Skill practice groups. In these groups the participants actually practice performing various skills of human relations and group participation, through role playing, case method, and other devices. Such skills as these are typically included: (1) diagnosing group problems, (2) being sensitive to the feelings of others and the needs of the group, (3) observing group interaction, (4) performing various member roles flexibly, (5) leading discussions, (6) interviewing, (7) planning meetings and workshops, and the like.

Simulation exercises. These are in effect mass role-playing exercises in which all participants experience the problems that arise in the relationships among the various kinds of groups in a hypothetical community.

A realistic community problem is described (such as whether or not to float a bond issue to build a new community college) in a hypothetical community. Then the learners are assigned to typical community groups that would be concerned with this problem (such as the PTA, the school board, the taxpayers' association, and the like) and they are instructed to act out what they would do to solve the problem. Trained observers collect data about the behavior of the participants as they become absorbed in the project. At the conclusion of the exercise the data are reported, and an analysis is made of what happened and why. Participative cases reinforce laboratory groups in helping people learn how to learn from analyzing their "here and now" behavior.

Project or production groups. Participants gain experience through these groups in planning and carrying out projects for the total laboratory or solving problems in which they are interested. Such projects include publishing a newsletter, conducting social events or large meetings, and preparing reports. These groups often provide opportunities to experiment with ways to improve group productivity.

Special-interest groups. Participants choose these groups according to their occupational or functional interests, such as supervision, board operation, staff management, membership recruitment, community organization, public relations, and the like. These groups are usually led by a specialist in the subject and have as their purpose the broadening and deepening of the participants' knowledge of a particular subject.

Application groups. These are small groups, often homogeneous in terms of occupation, geographic location, or institutional affiliation, that plan strategies for transferring their learnings from the laboratory to their back-home situation.

Organizational Development

In our 1959 edition of this little book we observed that "many of the ideas and techniques resulting from the study of group dynamics have infiltrated into the blood stream of American life and have exerted a subtle influence on the way groups and meetings are conducted. There seems to be a generally more democratic spirit developing in organizational life." We were apparently sensing at that time the beginning of a development which since then has flowered into a major type of social practice—*organization development* (often referred to as "OD").

Organization development represents a shift away from viewing collections of individuals to the viewing of total social systems as the "clients" (or targets of change) of human relations training.

Organization development is defined by three of its pioneering practitioners as follows:

By Bennis: "A complex educational strategy intended to change the beliefs, attitudes, values, and structures of organizations so they can better adapt to new technologies, markets, and challenges and the dizzying rate of change itself. . . . Changes sought are related directly to the demands the organization is trying to cope with . . . *i.e.,* problems of destiny, growth, identity and revitalization; problems of human satisfaction and development; and problems of organizational effectiveness." [4]

By Beckhard: "An effort, planned, organization-wide, and managed from the top to increase organizational effectiveness and health through planned interventions in the organizational processes using behavioral science knowledge." [5]

By Miles: "A planned and sustained effort to apply behavioral science for system improvement, using reflective, self-analytic methods." [6]

A number of corporations, government agencies, educational institutions, and national voluntary agencies have contracted with external "OD consultants" or have established internal "OD departments" to facilitate continuous processes of organizational self-renewal.

Indeed, a whole new profession of "change agents" is emerging to perform this role, with a growing body of literature to support them, of which the following are good examples (in addition to those cited in notes 4, 5 and 6 above):

Chris Argyris, *Intervention Theory and Method: A Behavioral Science View* (Reading, Mass.: Addison-Wesley, 1970).

Warren Bennis, Kenneth Benne, and Robert Chin, *The Planning of Change* (New York: Holt, Rinehart & Winston, 1968).

Edgar Schein, *Process Consultation: Its Role in Organization Development* (Reading, Mass.: Addison-Wesley, 1969).

Goodwin Watson (ed.), *Concepts for Social Change* (Washington, D.C.: NTL Institute of Applied Behavioral Science, 1967).

6

What Does It Add Up To?

THE field of group dynamics is too new for anyone to know what its ultimate status in the social sciences will be, or what its full contribution to society will be. There is some aura of controversy about it now. Perhaps this is because it is undermining old and comfortable ways of thinking about groups, or because of misconceptions about its nature and aims, or because it is inevitably making some mistakes in the process of pioneering uncharted territory. Or perhaps the critics of group dynamics are pointing to fundamental weaknesses and errors that need to be corrected. As you explore the literature of group dynamics, you might raise some of these questions that are posed by its critics, to see how it deals with them. We list the questions here along with our answers. (We give our own reactions primarily to clarify the meaning of the questions, not to prejudice your own search for answers.)

*Will the new knowledge and methods being un-
covered enable unscrupulous people to manipulate
groups more easily toward their selfish ends?*

Most knowledge can be used for good or evil, just
as a sharp axe can be used either to chop down a
tree or to chop off a man's head. We couldn't ban all
new knowledge that might be used for evil without
putting a stop to human progress. But in group dynamics there may be two built-in safeguards against
this danger: (1) The social scientists themselves are
acutely aware of their responsibility to accompany the
transmission of new knowledge and skills with ethical
undergirding. The literature is rich with examinations
of the ethical implication of their work and its relationship to the values of democratic society. And training
programs typically include periods for the examination of ethical questions. (2) Two of the essential
ingredients of group dynamics training are anti-manip-
ulative in their effect—training in shared leadership
and training in the collection and examination of data
about what is happening to the group.

*Isn't there a danger that all this emphasis on group
behavior will lead to a loss of individuality—that
"groupthink" will take over?*

To the social scientists this is almost the "unkindest
cut of all." For they know, from their study of groups,
that (1) as life becomes increasingly complex individuals become increasingly interdependent and must
inevitably do more and more of their work in groups,

and (2) nothing can be more tyrannical than a group whose members are unsophisticated about its dynamics. Indeed, probably the best way to preserve individuality is to give every individual the knowledge and skills necessary to diagnose and withstand the forces toward conformity and at the same time to express his individuality constructively. The leaders of group dynamics research and theory have made a special point of trying to disseminate their knowledge widely, and the leaders of applied group dynamics have made a point of training *all* group members, not just selected leaders.

Isn't the group dynamics field focusing too much attention on the process of groups at the expense of the content of their work?

Some critics are concerned that groups will become so introspective about their dynamic processes that they will lose sight of their real reasons for being—to produce ideas, pleasures, decisions, or other substantive products. The practitioners of applied group dynamics recognize that there is a danger, especially in the early stages of training, that this new dimension of group life might become so intriguing as to become an end in itself. They have tried to erect safeguards against its happening, including warning against it and pointing it out when it begins to occur. But this is a phenomenon that typically occurs only while people are actually in a training situation. In our experience the greater danger lies in a person's neglecting his newly learned skills of group-process observation once he returns home and becomes absorbed in the tasks of the groups to which he belongs.

Will not inexperienced or poorly trained people make use of techniques that might cause damage?

Since group dynamics brings into the open the part played by people's feelings in the life of a group, there is some danger that participants in a laboratory group might expose emotions too deep for leaders not trained in psychotherapy to handle. Applied group dynamics recognizes this danger, and builds cautions against it into both its literature and its training programs. Newly trained leaders are urged not to undertake the leadership of laboratory groups until they have served an apprenticeship under careful supervision, and have become skillful in preventing the traumatic overexposure of emotions. But this is an issue with which the leaders of the field have become increasingly concerned as its practitioners have proliferated. And, as this edition is going to press, a new organization has just come into being to make available to the public the credentials of approved trainers and consultants. It is the International Association of Applied Social Scientists, 1755 Massachusetts Avenue, Washington, D.C. 20036. Before entering into a program involving intensive group experience, readers are urged to examine the qualifications, training, and experience of the practitioners involved so as to assess their competence for the level of involvement expected.

Is there not a tendency for zealots to go all out for sensitivity training and to cast off other types of necessary training in specific processes and methods?

No doubt such a danger exists, and can be countered only by including in training programs consideration for the total range of training needs. But perhaps this is not too serious a tendency, at least for a while, if it is true that training in sensitivity to human relations has been so long neglected that there is a large gap to be made up.

Summing Up

In adding up the accomplishments of group dynamics to date it seems clear that the record is impressive. It has opened up new vistas of human potentiality that give promise of bringing about a social technology that will produce even greater miracles than those wrought by the material technology developed over the last century. It has accumulated a massive body of knowledge—more than we yet know how to use.

Important as have been the discoveries to date, it seems obvious to us that the surface has only been scratched. The years ahead are bound to bring further exciting developments, both in pushing back the frontiers of knowledge about human relations and in applying these unlocked secrets to practical human affairs. We look forward to an increasingly thrilling adventure in exploring new territories with the social scientists. And we hope our readers will join us on the trip.

Notes

1. Kurt Lewin, *Field Theory in Social Science*, Dorwin Cartwright, ed. (New York: Harper & Brothers, 1951), p. 169.
2. Paul Hare, Edgar Borgatta. and Robert Bales, *Small Groups* (New York: Alfred A. Knopf, Inc., 1955), pp. 2–3. By permission.
3. Kenneth D. Benne and Grace Levit, "The Nature of Groups and Helping Groups Improve Their Operation," *Review of Educational Research* (published by American Educational Research Association, Washington 6, D.C.), XXIII, No. 4 (October, 1953), p. 290. By permission.
4. Alvin W. Gouldner, *Studies in Leadership* (New York: Harper & Brothers, 1950), p. 25.
5. Kurt Lewin, *Field Theory in Social Science*, Dorwin Cartwright, ed. (New York: Harper & Brothers, 1951), p. 63. By permission.
6. Raymond B. Cattell, "New Concepts for Measuring Leadership in Terms of Group Syntality," *Human Relations*, 1951, VI, 163.
7. Ruth Strang, "Some Progress Has Been Made," *Readings in Group Work*, Dorothea Sullivan, ed. (New York: Association Press, 1952), p. 215.

8. A. Paul Hare, *Handbook of Small Group Research* (New York: The Free Press of Glencoe, 1962), p. vii.
9. Bertram H. Raven, *A Bibliography of Publications Relating to the Small Group* (Los Angeles: University of California Student Store, 1965).
10. Bertram H. Raven, *A Bibliography of Publications Relating to the Small Group* (Los Angeles: University of California Student Store, 1969).

CHAPTER 2

1. Dorothy Stock and Herbert A. Thelen, *Emotional Dynamics and Group Behavior* (Washington, D.C.: National Training Laboratories, 1958), pp. 22–33. By permission.

CHAPTER 3

1. Kenneth D. Benne and Paul Sheats, "Functional Roles of Group Members," *Journal of Social Issues,* Vol. IV, No. 2, Spring, 1948, p. 41.
2. Murray G. Ross and Charles E. Hendry, *New Understandings of Leadership* (New York: Association Press, 1957), p. 36. By permission.
3. See Harold Guetzkow, *Groups, Leadership and Men* (Pittsburgh: Carnegie Press, 1951).
4. The works cited, in order of their listing on the chart are: Herbert Thelen and Watson Dickerman, "Stereotypes and the Growth of Groups," *Educational Leadership,* 1949, pp. 6, 309–316.

M. B. Miles, "Human Relations Training: How a Group Grows," *Teachers College Record,* 1953, 55, pp. 90–96.

W. G. Bennis and H. A. Shepard, "A Theory of Group Development," *Human Relations,* 1956, 9, pp. 415–437.

William Schutz, *FIRO: A 3-Dimensional Theory of Interpersonal Behavior* (New York: Rinehart, 1958).

W. R. Bion, *Experiences in Groups* (New York: Basic Books, 1959).

R. T. Golembiewski, *The Small Group* (Chicago: University of Chicago Press, 1962).

L. P. Bradford, J. R. Gibb, and K. D. Benne, *T-Group Theory and Laboratory Method* (New York: John Wiley & Sons, 1964).

Theodore Mills, *Group Transformation* (Englewood Cliffs, N.J.: Prentice-Hall, 1964).

B. W. Tuckman, "Developmental Sequence in Small Groups," *Psychological Bulletin*, 1965, 63, pp. 384–399.

R. D. Mann *et al.*, *Interpersonal Styles and Group Development* (New York: John Wiley and Sons, Inc., 1967).

D. C. Dunphy, "Phase, Roles, and Myths of Self-Analytic Groups," *Journal of Applied Behavioral Science*, 1968, 4, pp. 195–225.

CHAPTER 4

1. Darwin Cartwright and Alvin Zander, *Group Dynamics Research and Theory* (Evanston, Ill.: Row, Peterson & Co., 1953), p. 4. By permission.
2. Dorothy Stock, "A Survey of Research on T-Groups," in L. P. Bradford, J. R. Gibb, and K. D. Benne (eds.), *T-Group Theory and Laboratory Method, op. cit.*, pp. 435–436.

CHAPTER 5

1. Herbert A. Thelen, *Dynamics of Groups at Work* (Chicago: University of Chicago Press, 1954), p. 181. Copyright 1954 by The University of Chicago. All rights reserved. By permission.
2. Leland P. Bradford, "An Approach to Human Relations Training," *Report of the Eleventh Summer Laboratory Sessions, Bethel, Maine, 1957* (Washington, D.C.: National Training Laboratories, 1957).
3. *Ibid.*

4. Warren Bennis, *Organization Development: Its Nature, Origins, and Prospects* (Reading, Mass.: Addison-Wesley, 1969), pp. 2–10.
5. Richard Beckhard, *Organization Development: Strategies and Models* (Reading, Mass.: Addison-Wesley, 1969), p. 3.
6. Matthew B. Miles, *Organization Development in Schools* (in preparation, 1971), p. 2.

Index